LOOK AT THAT SNOW G.B! ISN'T IT BEAUTIFUL!
I'LL TAKE YOUR WORD FOR IT.
SLURP!
CHOMP!
GULP!
JANUARY

IT'S HUMILIATING THAT'S WHAT IT IS . . .
SOLD FOR A HANDFUL OF SILVER -LIKE AN OLD SOFA!!
© Chris Moller
STILL, I SUPPOSE IT COULD BE WORSE . . .
MOST SOFAS DON'T GET GIVEN TITBITS !!

WELL WE'RE OFF TO MY NEW HOME
© Chris Moller
YOU'LL SEE I'M NOT LETTING THE TRAUMA OF MOVING GET TO ME!
I'M ENJOYING THE VIEW . . . HAVING A LEISURELY PULL AT MY HAYNET . . .
AND LEAVING THE WORRYING TO MY NEW 'PERSONAL HORSE-PERSON'!
FEED LIST
LIST OF TACK
PACE
PACE
TIME TABLE
PACE

SO THIS IS MY NEW HOME!
LOOK G.B.- A BRAND NEW STABLE FOR YOU! WARM... DRY...DEEP BED... SUPER VIEW...
WHEN YOU'VE QUITE FINISHED WITH THE SALES PITCH FOR THE ACCOMMODATION..
CAN WE GET ON TO MORE IMPORTANT MATTERS, -LIKE THE CATERING ARRANGEMENTS??
© Chris Moller

BANG!
BANG!!
BANG!!!
EEEEK!! G.B.'S GOT CAST IN HIS STABLE!!
PLEASE! DON'T PANIC!!
-I WAS ONLY SEEING IF THE KICKING-BOARDS WORKED!
© Chris Moller

RATTLE! RATTLE!!
HERE BOY!
HELLO! -THE OLD BUCKET OF NUTS TRICK,
HOPING THAT A BUCKET OF NUTS WILL PERSUADE ME TO LET MYSELF BE CAUGHT...
©Chris Moller
I ALWAYS WAS A MARTYR TO GREED!

OUR FIRST RIDE OUT TOGETHER...
AND I'M GOING TO BE ON MY BEST BEHAVIOUR,
©Chris Moller
-JUST AS LONG AS WE CAN COME TO AN AGREEMENT ON WHEN IT'S TIME TO TURN FOR HOME!

FEBRUARY

I'M OUT IN MY NEW FIELD AND THE SNOW'S DEEP AND CRISP AND EVEN
I FEEL ON TOP OF THE WORLD!
© Chris Moller
ALTHOUGH THIS FEELING OF LOFTY ELEVATION...
COULD BE PARTLY DUE TO THE BUILD-UP OF SNOW UNDER MY HOOVES!

HELLO! COMPANY!
I'M GORDON BENNET -WHO ARE YOU?
HELLO GORDON BENNET, THEY CALL ME SEABIRD
SEABIRD? SO YOU SOAR OVER JUMPS WITH ALL THE GRACE OF A GULL?
© Chris Moller
NO, 'COS I DIVE INTO MY FEED BUCKET WITH ALL THE GRACE OF A GANNET!!

AN ALL-WEATHER ARENA ? HOW DOES THAT WORK THEN ?
OH SIMPLE...
COME DROUGHT, DRIZZLE, RAIN, HAIL, SLEET, SNOW . . .
YOU'LL HAVE NO EXCUSE TO AVOID EXERCISING !!
©ChrisMoller

ALL THIS SNOW ! ISN'T IT EXCITING G.B !
IF IT KEEPS ON LIKE THIS WE'LL BE SNOWED IN !
-BE CUT OFF?? WE CAN'T BE!! CALL OUT THE R.A.F !!!
TELL THEM WE'RE DOWN TO OUR LAST PACKET OF POLOS !
©ChrisMoller

HELLO! I THOUGHT YOU AND SHE WERE GOING TO YOUR FIRST MEET TODAY?
NO...SOMETHING ABOUT THE FROST AND 'TOO MUCH BONE IN THE GROUND'.
BONES!!
WHERE??
WHERE??
WHERE??
WHERE??
WHERE??
WHERE?
©Chris Moller
IT'S OBVIOUSLY A MISTAKE TO MENTION B.O.N.E. TO A JACK RUSSELL

I KNOW SHE'S BUSY... BUT I WOULD APPRECIATE A QUICK WORD...
TO FIND OUT WHEN SUPPER WILL BE READY
EXCUSE ME!
NUDGE!
©Chris Moller
I HOPE I HAVEN'T CAUGHT YOU AT AN AWKWARD MOMENT...

VERY SOOTHING THIS GROOMING . . .
ZZZZZZ
!
OI !! WATCH WHERE YOU'RE GOING WITH THAT BRUSH!!
©Chris Moller

I MUST SAY I ENJOYED OUR FIRST DAY OUT HUNTING!
PITY WE HAD TO COME HOME EARLY..
©Chris Moller
JUST WHEN WE WERE GOING SO WELL . . .
WE WERE BEATING THE MASTER AND THE REST BY MILES !!

MARCH

HELLO! THAT LOOKS SUS-PICIOUSLY LIKE AN 'EXPERT'
'HERE'S THE EXERCISE PROGRAM I'VE DRAWN UP
I SINCERELY HOPE THAT'S FOR HER, NOT ME . . .
I COULD DO WITH CARRYING A LITTLE LESS OF HER ABOUT!

OH NO! BATHTIME!!
BRRR! IT'S STILL FAR TOO EARLY! IT STILL FEELS LIKE WINTER OUTSIDE MY RUG!!
-IF SHE DOESN'T WARM THAT WATER . . .
I'LL SHOW HER THE NAIL HEADS ON MY HIND SHOES!!

WHAT'S THE MATTER WITH G.B.?
OH I DECIDED TO BORROW SOME CLIPPERS AND HAVE A GO MYSELF
TROUBLE IS IT TURNED OUT NOT SO MUCH A TRACE CLIP...
MORE A 'SORRY' WITH A FRINGE ON TOP!
©Chris Moller

HELLO! WHAT'S THIS?
©Chris Moller
LOOK G.B.! ISN'T IT LOVELY! IT WAS AN ABSOLUTE BARGAIN! ONLY ONE OWNER . . .
OUR VERY OWN TRANSPORT!
TRANSPORT?? -LOOKS MORE LIKE A RUBBISH SKIP!!

I MUST SAY I'M ENJOYING THIS
NEW GAME OF 'LOAD-THE-HORSE' . . .
SO FAR I'M AHEAD TWO AND THREE !
©Chris Moller
TWO AND THREE?
TWO HOURS AND THREE BUCKETS OF NUTS !!

I WILL HAVE TO
LODGE A PROTEST !
CHOMP!
CHOMP!
©Chris Moller
WHEN PLAYING 'LOAD-THE-HORSE'
CHOMP!
IT'S A DELIBERATE FOUL . . .
TO PUT MY BREAKFAST IN THE TRAILER !

C'MON BOY PLEEASE !!
NOT UNTIL WE'VE DISCUSSED WHAT'S IN IT FOR ME . . .
HOW MANY EXTRA POLOS?!
BRIBERY IS AN UGLY WORD, -I PREFER TO CALL IT A PERFORMANCE-RELATED BONUS !!
©Chris Moller

I MUST SAY THIS JUMPING LARK IS QUITE FUN -APART FROM OUR 'THREE POINT LANDINGS'. . .
ONE, MY FORE END. . .
TWO, MY HIND END. . .
THREE, - OOOF! HER REAR END !!
©Chris Moller

APRIL
WHAT! NO BREAKFAST??!
SORRY G.B! I'M AFRAID WE'VE RUN OUT!
HA! HA! -APRIL FOOL!!
VERY HUMOROUS!! APRIL FOOL INDEED!! -JUST WAIT 'TILL SHE GETS ON BOARD...
CHOMP!
CHOMP!
WE'LL SEE WHO'S THIS APRIL'S FOOL!!

HELLO! NO EXERCISE THIS MORNING?
NO, I LOST A SHOE OUT IN MY FIELD. -WHILE WE WAIT FOR THE BLACKSMITH,
SHE'S GONE TO LOOK FOR IT...
YIPES!!
OH GOOD! I THINK SHE'S FOUND IT!!

THIS GAME OF 'LOAD-THE-HORSE' COULD BECOME BORING . . .
SO I THINK I'LL LIVEN IT UP BY WORKING OUT. . .
©Chris Moller
WHEN SHE'S IN A PANIC TO GET TO A SHOW . . .
OR LIKE NOW, JUST PRACTISING!!
GOOD BOY!!

I'M NOT SO SURE ABOUT THIS 'ROADWORK'
OUR EXPERT TOLD US IT'S ESSENTIAL
FOR BUILDING UP OUR MUSCLES . . .
BUT-COUGH!-I DREAD TO THINK WHAT IT'S DOING TO OUR LUNGS !!
©Chris Moller

©ChrisMoller
MORNING G.B!!
BANG! BANG!
RATTLE!
CHARGE
YE GODS! DOESN'T SHE KNOW IT'S STILL OFFICIALLY NIGHT!!
RSSSP!
RUSH!
CLATTER!
ROUND HERE, THE EARLY BIRD JUST GETS THE RASPBERRY!!

THE ONLY THING TO BE SAID . . .
REGARDING THESE NAUSEATING BURSTS OF EARLY-MORNING ENTHUSIASM . . .
AND MERRIMENT, IS THAT THEY DON'T TEND . . .
©ChrisMoller
TO LAST VERY LONG!
ZZZZ

MOST EXCITING! OFF TO OUR FIRST 'DO' . . .
©Chris Moller
THOUGH I CAN'T HELP
LURCH!
WORRYING . . .
SWAY!
THAT WE MAY HAVE
BUMP!
FORGOTTEN
BUMP! BUMP!!
SOMETHING,
-LIKE PERHAPS THE DIRECTIONS?
FOOTPATH ONLY

HOME AT LAST,
HOME FROM OUR FIRST COMPETITION!
OWDOWN STABLES
POSITIVELY COVERED -WELL NOT EXACTLY IN GLORY . . .
© Chris Moller
BUT IT WAS HARDLY MY FAULT IF, JUST WHERE I HAPPENED TO PUT IN A LITTLE STOP,
THERE HAD BEEN SOME VERY LOOSE COWS!!

MAY

A GLORIOUS SUNNY DAY WITH JUST ENOUGH BREEZE TO KEEP THE FLIES OFF . . .
IT'S SAD!
AND HER CHOOSING TO SPEND IT. .
DOWN BY THE GATE WITH A BUCKET . . .
HOPING THAT A HANDFUL OF NUTS 'LL PERSUADE ME TO GO AND POUND ROUND A HOT DUSTY ARENA !
C'MON G.B.!
HERE BOY!!
SHAKE!!
SHAKE!!

NOW WHAT'S SHE UP TO ?
BRUSH . . . COMB . . .
NEEDLE AND THREAD ?!?
HERE WE GO – FIVE MINUTES FIDDLING AND RE-THREADING BEFORE GOING TO LOOK FOR THE PLAITING-BANDS!
© Chris Moller

IT'S QUITE UNFAIR!
OUR FIRST PROPER 'DO' AND I'M COOPED UP IN HERE . . .
IT BEING NOT DONE FOR ME TO 'TALK' TO THE OTHER COMPETITORS . . .
©Chris Moller
WHILE SHE HASN'T STOPPED SINCE WE GOT HERE !!
YAKITY! YAKITY! YAKITY! YAKITY!
YAKITY! YAKITY!

I MUST ADMIT THAT, SEEING ALL THESE OTHER COMPETITORS . . .
HER EFFORTS ON MY MANE . . .
©Chris Moller
ALTHOUGH STILL TECHNICALLY PLAITS . .
MIGHT BETTER BE DESCRIBED AS DREADLOCKS !

HELLO! HOW DID YOU GET ON AT YOUR FIRST PROPER 'DO'?
FIRST
MODEST
© Chris Moller
WOW! YOU CAME FIRST!?!
UM, NO, NOT CAME FIRST, -ELIMINATED AT THE FIRST!

I SAY! I KNOW WE WERE LATE LEAVING . . .
BUT SHE'S GOING A BIT FAST FOR MY LIKING!!
LURCH!
SWAY!
BUMP!
RATTLE!
© Chris Moller
EEEK!!
NOTHING LIKE A LITTLE SYNCHRONISED WEIGHT-TRANSFER FOR SLOWING 'EM DOWN!!
CREEP
CRAWL

OH G.B.!
WHAT AN AWFUL ROUND!
CLEAR ROUND JUMPING
©Chris Moller
YOU SMASHED THROUGH EVERY SINGLE ONE!!
ME!?! I LIKE THAT!! -IT MIGHT HAVE HELPED IF YOU HAD EVEN GIVEN..
A VAGUE IMPRESSION THAT YOU WERE DOING THE SAME ROUND AS ME!!!

AS YOU CAN GATHER,
SHE'S CHANGED OUR ROUTINE...
IN DURING THE DAY AND OUT AT NIGHT 'COS OF THE FLIES...
WHICH SEEMS A BIT POINTLESS SINCE ALL THE FLIES ROUND HERE...
©Chris Moller
SEEM TO HAVE ADOPTED THE SAME ROUTINE!
BUZZ
BUZZ
BUZZ
BUZZ

JUNE
I MUST SAY I ENJOY EARLY MORNING EXERCISE!
THE SUN RISING ON A FRESH NEW DAY...
TURNING EACH DEW-SOAKED SPIDER'S WEB INTO A NECKLACE OF DIAMONDS,
AND HER STILL TOO DOZY TO WANT TO DO ANYTHING ENERGETIC!!
YAWN!
© Chris Moller

GOOD OF HER TO FORGET TO SHOOT THE BOLT ON MY DOOR - I ENJOYED MY LITTLE BIT OF FREEDOM!
JUST LOOK AT OUR LAWN! IT'S RUINED!!
© Chris Moller
OH DEAR! IF THEY'RE GOING TO BE LIKE THAT ABOUT THE LAWN
JUST WHAT ARE THEY GOING TO SAY ABOUT THE FLOWERBEDS??

SHE'S REALLY GOT TO DO SOMETHING ABOUT HER OLD LAND ROVER !
IF THERE'S ONE PART OF GOING TO A 'DO' I DREAD, -IT'S THESE LONG HILLS !
-AND ALL THE FOUL LOOKS AND COMMENTS FROM THE QUEUE OF TRAFFIC WHEN THEY FINALLY MANAGE TO GET PAST US !!
© Chris Moller
— AND THE CYCLISTS ARE THE WORST !

OH DEAR ME !
SHE SHOULD KNOW HOW I FEEL ABOUT WATER...
AND THAT I WOULD WANT TO STOP AND CHECK IT OUT FIRST . . .
© Chris Moller
BUT NO, SHE HAS TO KEEP RIGHT ON GOING !

PHEW! THROUGH THE WATER AT LAST!!
C'MON BOY HOME! AND LET'S MAKE UP SOME TIME!!!
HOME A.S.A.P!! -RIGHT BOSS!!
©Chris Moller
RELAX! AND LEAVE IT TO ME...
I KNOW A SHORTCUT!
COME BACK!!
13

WHAT A DISASTER!! THREE SEPARATE 'STOPS'... A DUCKING AT THE WATER...
OH G.B.! SOB!
MISSING THE LAST HALF OF THE COURSE... THE CLUB WONT WANT US BACK AGAIN!!
OH YOU DONT HAVE TO WORRY ABOUT BEING OUT OF THE CLUB...
©Chris Moller
I DISTINCTLY HEARD THE SECRETARY SAY SHE HADN'T HAD SUCH A LAUGH IN AGES!!

LOOK AT ALL
THAT OLD HORSE-DRAWN FARM MACHINERY G.B.!
RURAL MUSEUM
WOULDN'T IT BE FUN IF WE COULD MAKE OUR OWN HAY !?
©Chris Moller
HORSE DRAWN??
FUN FOR WHOM PRAY?

WELL THAT'S IT!
WE CAN KISS GOODBYE TO THE FINE WEATHER...
©Chris Moller
AND IT'S ALL HER FAULT–AT THIS TIME OF THE YEAR SHE SHOULD KNOW BETTER...
THAN TO EVEN MENTION HAYMAKING!!
RUMBLE!

JULY
CALL ME SOFT IF YOU LIKE . . .
GIVING UP ON A GAME OF 'CATCH-AS-CATCH-CAN' ROUND MY FIELD . . .
BUT I JUST CAN'T BEAR TO SEE A GROWN HORSE-PERSON CRY !!
© Chris Moller
WELL, THE BLACKSMITH'S GETTING READY . . .
HEATING UP HIS PORTABLE FURNACE . . .
'THOUGH I HAVE TO ADMIT THAT I PREFER COLD SHOEING . . .
© Chris Moller
AT LEAST THEN WE CAN ALL SEE WHAT WE'RE DOING !!
COUGH!
COUGH !
COUGH!

SHE SHOULD KNOW I DON'T THINK MUCH OF THIS WORMING LARK!
PTOOOI!!!
© Chris Moller
BUT YOU HAVE TO GIVE HER CREDIT. . .
FOR PERSEVERANCE!!

HI! HOW DID YOU AND G.B. DO ON THE SHOW-JUMPING?
MOST PLEASING THANK YOU! I WAS IN GREAT FORM! -CLEARED EVERYTHING IN SIGHT! ACCORDING TO THE JUDGES: EXCELLENT!!
DISASTER!! THE LITTLE S.O.D CARTED ME!! -TOOK ALL THE WRONG JUMPS!!
© Chris Moller
SO THE 'E' AGAINST MY NAME ON THE SCOREBOARD DOESN'T STAND FOR EXCELLENT???

I DON'T KNOW ABOUT THIS NEW FLY FRINGE SHE'S GOT ME . . .
ALTHOUGH THERE'S NO DOUBTING IT'S EFECTIVENESS . . .
IT'S DRAWING THE LITTLE BLIGHTERS FROM MILES AROUND!!
© Chris Moller

WELL IT'S ABOUT TIME SHE GOT AROUND TO CLEANING OUT MY WATER-TROUGH!
THE WATER IN THERE WAS GETTING TO THE STAGE. . .
WHERE I DIDN'T KNOW WHETHER TO DRINK IT . . .
OR EAT IT !!
© Chris Moller

WELL! WE FINALLY DID IT! WE COMPLETED THE CROSS-COUNTRY COURSE!!
AND LOOK! HERE'S OUR SECRETARY HURRYING OVER...
NO DOUBT TO CONGRATULATE US ON OUR ACHIEVEMENT!
EVERYONE ELSE LEFT AN HOUR AGO... CLOSE THE GATE BEHIND YOU!!
TRIAL
©Chris Moller

SO! YOU'RE OFF TO PONY CLUB CAMP THEN?
I REMEMBER HAVING A GREAT TIME - APART FROM HARDLY GETTING A WINK OF SLEEP!
WHAT? WITH THE LITTLE DEVILS TALKING ALL NIGHT?
-YES, THAT, AND THE CLINKING OF EMPTY CIDER BOTTLES!!
©Chris Moller

AUGUST
TRA LA! SHE SAID. WE'RE OFF ON OUR HOLS! SHE SAID.
LOTS OF RIDES AND PRACTICE AND COMPETITION! SHE SAID.
SHE MAY BE LOOKING FORWARD TO THIS 'HOLIDAY'...
BUT IT SOUNDS OMINOUSLY LIKE A LOT OF HARD WORK FOR YOURS TRULY!
©Chris Moller
WELL I MUST ADMIT THIS 'HOLIDAY' IS OK! - A STROLL ALONG THE SUNNY SANDS...
-A REFRESHING DIP IN THE SPARKLING WATERS...
OI! WATCH WHERE YOU'RE GOING YOU DOZY GROCKLE!!
AND A CHEERY WORD WITH ONE OF THE LOCALS!!
©Chris Moller

EXCITING THIS! - JUST LIKE ONE OF THOSE DESERT FILMS!
THE SUN BLAZING DOWN ON THE BURNING SAND!
©Chris Moller
- WILL OUR HEROS MAKE IT . . .
TO THE NEXT ICE CREAM STALL??

AND NOW FOLKS, FOR OUR NEXT TRICK . . .
SCHOOLING IN THE DESERT . . .
©Chris Moller
ROUND AND ROUND IN EVER-DECREASING CIRCLES . . .
'TILL WE DISAPPEAR UP OUR OWN HEAT-HAZE!!

I BLAME THIS HOT WEATHER DOWN HERE AT THE SEASIDE...
©Chris Moller
FOR US COLLECTING SO MANY TIME PENALTIES...
BUT IT REALLY WAS MOST REFRESHING...
TO SPEND A BIT OF TIME COOLING OFF IN THAT WATER-JUMP!
GB

I SAY !! OLD G.B.'S BEEN ON GOOD PASTURE ON HIS HOLS EH? HEH! HEH!
ZZZ
©Chris Moller
SHHH!! HE MIGHT HEAR YOU!
NONSENSE! HE'S FAST ASLEEP. BESIDES, HE'S NOT SENSITIVE ABOUT HIS WEIGHT IS HE?
ZZZ
HE WILL BE AS SOON AS HE FINDS OUT HE'S BEEN PUT ON A D.I.E.T !!

HELP ! THE NEW HAY'S ARRIVED, THE STORE'S NOT READY AND IT LOOKS LIKE RAIN . . .
WE'LL JUST HAVE TO PUT IT IN G.B.'S STABLE – IT WON'T HURT HIM TO BE OUT FOR ONE NIGHT !
HELLO !! JUST LOOK AT MY STABLE !!
I KNOW I LIKE A FULL HAY-NET AT NIGHT, BUT THAT'S RIDICULOUS !
©Chris Moller

A FINE THING !
– ME STUCK OUT HERE . . .
'COS THEY HAD TO PUT THE NEW HAY IN MY STABLE IN CASE IT RAINS !
WHEN WE COULD BOTH BE IN THERE . .
I COULD HAVE EATEN MY WAY IN !
©Chris Moller

SEPTEMBER
I THINK SHE MIGHT BE A BIT OPTIMISTIC . . .
OUT LOOKING FOR MUSHROOMS IN MY FIELD . . .
I CAN'T STAND THE THINGS . . .
SO I TREAD 'EM ALL IN!
© Chris Moller

IF THERE'S ANY COMPEN-SATION FOR BEING BACK 'IN' . . .
IT'S THE GRUB SITUATION . . .
OUT IN MY FIELD I WAS WEARING MY HOOVES OUT TRYING TO FIND ENOUGH GRUB TO KEEP BODY AND SOUL TOGETHER!
IT'S GOOD TO HAVE SOME-ONE ELSE DOING ALL THE LEGWORK!
© Chris Moller

HELLO ! WHAT'S THIS ?
SO SHE'S LASHED OUT AND GOT HERSELF A BACK-PROTECTOR . . .
©Chris Moller
NO DOUBT TO LOOK THE COMPLETE PROFESSIONAL,
-ROLL ON THE DAY WHEN SHE RIDES LIKE ONE !!

AH! HERE'S MY BLACKSMITH . . .
IN HIS SMART NEW VAN -MOST APPROPRIATE, BLACK WITH GOLD LETTERING . . .
FARRIER
TEL: 65431
THE BLACK IS OF COURSE FOR BLACKSMITH . . .
©Chris Moller
AND THE GOLD FOR THE SIZE OF HIS BILL !!

SO! THAT MUST BE HER FRIEND'S NEW STALLION SHE'S BEEN GOING ON ABOUT!
HE DOESN'T LOOK THAT SPECIAL TO ME . . .
AS FAR AS I CAN SEE HE'S ONLY GOT ONE THING OVER ME!
WELL, TO BE PRECISE, TWO !!
© Chris Moller

I MUST SAY I'M JUST BEGINNING TO GET THE HANG OF THIS 'CROSS-COUNTRY'
© Chris Moller
IT'S A BIT LIKE THOSE WRESTLING MATCHES!
THERE! I THINK I WIN BY TWO FALLS . . .
AND ONE SUBMISSION!
THAT'S IT! I'VE HAD ENOUGH!!

IT'S MOST UNFAIR!
I WAS RUDELY EJECTED! BANISHED!! THROWN OUT!!! FORCIBLY REMOVED!!!!
AND I ONLY PEEPED INTO THE FEED STORE..
TO SEE WHAT WAS ON TONIGHT'S MENU . . .
TEA
LUNCH
© Chris Moller

I KNOW SHE'S STILL CROSS ABOUT THE FEED STORE . . .
ONE...
TWO...
BUT I'D HAVE THOUGHT SHE'S MADE HER POINT BY JUST GIVING ME NUTS FOR TEA,
THREE...
FOUR...
WITHOUT RUBBING IT IN . . .
FIVE...
SIX...
BY COUNTING THEM OUT ONE BY ONE!
SEVEN..
EIGHT...
RIGHT! THAT'S ENOUGH!
© Chris Moller

OCTOBER
OH G.B! JUST LOOK AT YOUR RUG - YOU'VE TORN IT !!
NO NO! NOT THE SPARE !!
SIGH! I'LL JUST HAVE TO DIG OUT THAT OLD SPARE!
LAST TIME I WORE THAT 'SPARE' SHE WOULDN'T STOP LAUGHING . . .
AND REFERING TO ME AS 'WORZEL'!!
HELLO G.B. . . .
I THOUGHT YOU WERE ASHAMED TO BE SEEN IN THAT OLD SPARE RUG !?
I'M *HOPING* SOMEONE WILL SEE. . .
AND REPORT HER FOR MENTAL CRUELTY !!
©Chris Moller

I'VE SENT YOUR RUG AWAY FOR REPAIR G.B. AND ASKED IF THEY CAN LET IT OUT,
OH DEAR! SHE'S IN ONE OF THOSE MOODS, NOW FOLLOWS A HUMOROUS REFERENCE TO THE WEIGHT I'M SUPPOSED TO HAVE PUT ON OVER THE SUMMER...
© Chris Moller
- BUT THEY WEREN'T SURE IF THEY HAD ENOUGH MATERIAL IN THE WAREHOUSE!!
OH HA HA! VERY DROLL! -WE'LL SEE WHO'S STILL LAUGHING WHEN THE BILL COMES IN!
CACKLE! CACKLE!

OH YES! I'M VERY PLEASED WITH MY TRAILER...
HEY! OUR TRAILER IF YOU DON'T MIND!
OURS! OR TO BE MORE PRECISE, MINE, HER'S...
© Chris Moller
AND THE BANK'S!!

AHAH ! SO THIS IS THE LAUNCH OF HER NEW ENTERPRISE !
-AN IDEA SHE GOT FROM OUR FARMER NEXT DOOR . . .
'THOUGH I AM A LITTLE DOUBTFUL WHETHER HERS HAS THE SAME APPEAL...
AS HIS STRAWBERRIES !!
©Chris Moller
PICK • YOUR OWN MANURE

LIFE IS VERY STRESS-FUL ! DECISIONS , ALL THE TIME DECISIONS!
I LIKE GOING HUNTING . . .
BUT NOT WHEN WE STAND AROUND ALL DAY WHILE SHE 'COFFEE-HOUSES'
©Chris Moller
TO BE OR NOT TO BE, LOADED, THAT IS THE QUESTION !
PLEASE BOY ! PLEEEASE !!

I KNEW I WAS RIGHT TO BE DOUBTFUL ABOUT OUR DAY'S HUNTING...
WHAT WITH ALL THE RAIN, WE'VE HAD TO SPEND ALL DAY ON THE ROAD . . .
UP AND DOWN ! BACK AND FORTH! TO AND FRO !
WE'LL PROBABLY GET A BILL FROM THE COUNCIL FOR REPAIRS!
©ChrisMolleR

I KNOW IT'S THE END OF THE SEASON . . .
BUT WOULD YOU JUST LOOK AT THE STATE OF HER !!
-BRINGS A WHOLE NEW MEANING...
TO THE TERM 'ROUGHING-OFF'!!
©ChrisMolleR

NOVEMBER
WICKER! WICKER!
I SAY! ISN'T HE JUST A SWEETIE !!
OH YES - ISN'T HE A DEAR! I MUST GET HIM AN APPLE!
EVERY TIME A COCONUT! - OR IN THIS CASE, AN APPLE !!
© Chris Moller

OH DEAR! HER EXPERT HAS TOLD HER THAT SHE SHOULD REMOVE . . .
ALL 'AHEM' FROM MY FIELD DAILY . . .
AND THERE SHE IS! - HOW EMBARRASSING!
WHY NOT JUST HANG THE BUCKET UNDER MY TAIL !?!
© Chris Moller

OH !
THIS AWFUL WEATHER !! ARE YOU COLD BOY ?
OH YES !!
SHIVVER SHAKE SHIVVER SHAKE SHIVVER
GOODNESS ! POOR OLD G.B! YOU'D BETTER COME IN !!
ACTUALLY IT'S NOT TOO BAD UNDER MY RUG...
BUT I NEVER MISS A CHANCE FOR A SPOT OF TEA AND SYMPATHY !

OH DEAR !
A NICE FINE DAY FOR OUR RIDE AND SHE'S IN ONE OF HER MOODS !
WELL ! TWO CAN PLAY AT THAT GAME...
AHHHHHH !
EEEEEK !
RUSTLE
RUSTLE
NOW THAT, FOR A START IS MY SILLY MOOD . . .

OH G.B.! HOW COULD YOU!
ME! I LIKE THAT!!
©Chris Moller
EVERY ONE DOWN! THAT WAS EVEN WORSE THAN LAST TIME!!
IT MIGHT HELP IF YOU WERE ABLE TO JOIN ME OVER A JUMP OCCASIONALLY!

HERE WE ARE BOY!
NUDGE!!
YOU SILLY BOY! WHY DO YOU ALWAYS DO THAT?
©Chris Moller
I COULD ASK THE SAME ABOUT SOME OF YOUR LITTLE HABITS!

ISN'T THAT SWEET ! OLD G.B. AND SEABIRD TALKING TO EACH OTHER . . .
THEY SAY THEY USE TELEPATHY !
TELEPATHY ? -NONSENSE ! WATCH THE EARS...
IT'S SEMAPHORE !!
©Chris Moller

HELLO ! WHAT'S UP ?
BLAST !!
OH DEAR ! LOOKS LIKE SHE'S CAST A SHOE . . .
HOP !
HOP !
HOP !
SHE WANT'S TO HAVE WORDS WITH THAT BLACKSMITH...
ABOUT NAILING 'EM ON BETTER !
©Chris Moller

DECEMBER

WHAT ON EARTH ARE YOU DOING G.B.?
CAN'T YOU SEE? TRYING TO CATCH RAINDROPS,
-AND DRAWING YOUR ATTENTION TO THE FACT...
THAT MY WATER BUCKET'S EMPTY!
©Chris Moller

OH G.B.! JUST LOOK AT THE STATE OF YOU!! WHY MUST YOU ROLL??
IT'S INSTINCT! MUD GETS RID OF PARASITES, KEEPS OFF FLIES,
PROTECTS ME FROM THE WEATHER...
AND POSTPONES THE START OF SCHOOLING!
©Chris Moller

WELL! OUR FIRST DAY OUT WITH A BIG HUNT!
HORSES
AND I'M WEARING A GREEN TAIL-RIBBON TO SHOW THAT I'M A NOVICE.
HAVE YOU SEEN THE SIZE OF SOME OF THOSE HEDGES G.B.?? THEY'RE ABSOLUTELY MASSIVE!!!
!
©Chris Moller
ER..PERHAPS WE SHOULD CHANGE THE TAIL-RIBBON FOR A YELLOW ONE??

OH YES! WE HAD A SUPER DAY OUT HUNTING!!
AND WE JUMPED THE HUGEST HEDGE YOU'VE EVER SEEN!!
©Chris Moller
ER YES...THAT WAS WHEN WE WERE LOOKING FOR THE EASY WAY...
AND GOT PINNED BETWEEN TWO MEMBERS OF THE PONY CLUB!

HELLO! WHAT'S SHE UP TO ?
I'M HANGING UP YOUR CHRISTMAS STOCKING G.B.!-FOR SANTA TO FILL WITH PRESENTS!!
GOSH! A LITTLE STOCKING FOR MY PRESENTS!
IF SANTA EXPECTS A HAPPY CHRISTMAS RIDING I WOULD SUGGEST SOMETHING A BIT BIGGER..
© Chris Moller

WELL! THIS 'CHRISTMAS' IS ALRIGHT!
LOTS OF GOODIES IN MY STOCKING, AND NOW A SPECIAL FEED . . .
MERRY XMAS
ALTHOUGH I HAVE TO ADMIT THAT THE BITS ROUND THE OUTSIDE . . .
DON'T HAVE MUCH FLAVOUR!
© Chris Moller

VERY FETCHING, THE NEW STETSON AND COWBOY BOOTS . . .
I'M TRYING TO REMEMBER WHICH WESTERN CHAR-ACTER SHE REMINDS ME OF . . .
© Chris Moller
T·RIP !!
AH YES ! CALAMITY JANE !!

SO ! A NEW YEAR DAWNS AND SHE'S FULL OF RESOLUTIONS FOR THE COMING MONTHS . . .
STRICT DIET
MORE EXERCISE
PRACTICE
TRAINING
FITNESS
TUITION
© Chris Moller
AND I'M GOING TO DO MY BEST TO HELP HER . . .
BREAK THEM ALL IN RECORD TIME !